Nonfiction Classics for Students, Volume 4

Project Editor
David Galens

Editorial
Sara Constantakis, Anne Marie Hacht, Michael
L. LaBlanc, Ira Mark Milne, Pam Revitzer,
Jennifer Smith, Daniel Toronto, Carol Ullmann
Permissions
Kim Davis, Debra Freitas **Manufacturing**
Stacy Melson

Imaging and Multimedia
Lezlie Light, Kelly A. Quin, Luke Rademacher
Product Design
Pamela A. E. Galbreath, Michael Logusz © 2002 by
Gale. Gale is an Imprint of The Gale Group, Inc., a
division of Thomson Learning Inc.

For more information, contact

The Gale Group, Inc.
27500 Drake Rd.
Farmington Hills, MI 48331-3535
Or you can visit our Internet site at
http://www.gale.com

While every effort has been made to ensure the reliability of the information presented in this publication, The Gale Group, Inc. does not guarantee the accuracy of the data contained herein. The Gale Group, Inc. accepts no pay-ment for listing; and inclusion in the publication of any organization, agency, institution, publication, service, or individual does not imply endorsement of the editors or publisher. Errors brought to the attention of the publisher and verified to the satisfaction of the publisher will be corrected in future editions.

ISBN 0-7876-6033-7
ISSN 1533-7561

Printed in the United States of America
10 9 8 7 6 5 4 3 2 1

Black Lamb and Grey Falcon: A Journey through Yugoslavia

Rebecca West

1941

Introduction

From 1936 to 1938, journalist and novelist Rebecca West made three trips to Yugoslavia. *Black Lamb and Grey Falcon: A Journey through Yugoslavia* is a record of her travels. This immensely long book, which runs to 1150 pages, is much more than a travelogue, however. It is also a vivid account of the violent history of the Balkans going back many hundreds of years. West admits that before she visited the region, she knew almost nothing about it, other than that events in the Balkans (notably the assassination of Austria's Archduke Franz Ferdinand in 1914) had led to World War I. Since the war had affected West's own life—as it had all members of West's generation—she wanted to understand how and why it happened. Her aim in writing *Black Lamb and Grey Falcon* was to show the Balkan past alongside the present it created.

In her travels, West became an admirer of the Serbs and their culture, often contrasting it favorably with the West. She repeatedly refers to the devastation that followed the famous battle of Kossovo in 1389, in which the Serbs were defeated by the Turks, and which led to five hundred years of Turkish rule. (In modern spelling, one "s" for Kosovo is preferred, rather than West's "Kossovo".) In the epilogue (written in 1941, two years after the outbreak of World War II) she praised Yugoslavia for refusing to capitulate to Nazi Germany.

In addition to being a travelogue and a history, *Black Lamb and Grey Falcon* is a forum for West's forcefully argued views on a variety of topics, ranging from relations between men and women, to art and music, to the nature of empires and questions of metaphysics. The book in some sections resembles a novel. It illustrates the relationship between West and her husband, and contains a lively cast of traveling companions, including Constantine (the Jewish Serb poet) and Gerda (his nationalistic German wife).

Author Biography

Rebecca West was born Cicily Isabel Fairfield on December 21, 1892, in London, England. Her father was Charles Fairfield, a former army officer, and her mother, Isabella MacKenzie Fairfield, was a pianist. Cicily Fairfield spent her early years in London, England, and was then educated at George Watson's Ladies' College in Edinburgh, Scotland. She also studied at the Academy of Dramatic Art in London. In 1911 she joined the suffragist movement and became a book reviewer for the *Freewoman,* a feminist magazine. In the same year she adopted the name Rebecca West. In 1913 West became a political writer for the socialist magazine, the *Clarion.* She was ready to embark on her distinguished career as novelist, literary critic, journalist, and biographer.

In 1916, West's study of the writer Henry James was published. Two years later her first novel, *The Return of the Soldier*, appeared, followed in 1922 by a second novel, *The Judge*. In 1923 she went on a lecture tour in the United States. She returned to the United States in 1926, and began reviewing books for the *New York Herald Tribune.*

In 1928 West published a collection of literary essays titled *The Strange Necessity*, followed by books on D. H. Lawrence (1930) and St. Augustine (1933), and a third novel, *The Thinking Reed* (1936). In the mid-1930s, West made three trips to the Balkans, which resulted in *Black Lamb and Grey Falcon: A Journey through Yugoslavia* (1941). During World War II West was asked to supervise the British Broadcasting Corporation's wartime broadcasts to Yugoslavia. After the war, West attended the Nuremberg war crimes trials in 1946—an experience she discusses in *A Train of Powder* (1955)—and wrote a nonfiction work titled *The Meaning of Treason* (1947).

In 1953, West wrote a series of controversial articles for the London *Sunday Times* in which she downplayed the damaging consequences of McCarthyism in the United States. This work came as a surprise to many since West had previously supported liberal points of view and defended civil liberties.

A novel called *The Fountain Overflows* was published in 1956, followed by the literary essays in *The Court and the Castle* (1957), consisting mainly of West's Terry Lectures at Yale University. West wrote about a spy scandal in Britain in *The Vassall Affair* (1963), and then returned to fiction in *The Birds Fall Down* (1966). In 1982 *1900*, a social history of the year 1900, was published. The novels *This Real Night* (1984) and *Cousin Rosamund* (1985) were published posthumously.

West was awarded numerous honors, including the Order of St. Sava in 1937, the Women's Press Club Award for Journalism in 1948, Companion of the British Empire (CBE) in 1949, and Chevalier of the Legion of Honor in 1957. She was named Dame Commander of the Order of the British Empire

(DBE) in 1959.

West had one child, Anthony (born in 1914), by H. G. Wells, whom she met in 1913 and had a close relationship with for ten years. In 1930 West married Henry Maxwell Andrews, a banker and investment counselor, who died in 1968. West died in London on March 15, 1983, of pneumonia, at the age of ninety.

Plot Summary

Prologue

In the prologue to *Black Lamb and Grey Falcon*, West explains how she came to be interested in Yugoslavia. She recalls her distress when she heard in 1934 that King Alexander of Yugoslavia had been assassinated in Marseille. At that point, West knew nothing of Yugoslavia, other than the fact that the Balkans was a violent place. But given the fact that events in the Balkans led to World War I, in which West as a British citizen had been endangered, her ignorance of the region meant that she knew nothing about her own destiny. In 1936 she was invited to lecture in Yugoslavia, and the following year she visited the country again.

Journey

West and her husband travel by train from Salzburg, Austria, to Zagreb, the capital of Croatia. Traveling in a first-class carriage, they meet some disagreeable Germans, who force a young man to vacate his seat because he only has a second-class ticket. It later transpires that the Germans have second-class tickets too.

Croatia

In Zagreb they meet three friends: Constantine, a Serb poet; Valetta, a Croat mathematician; and Marko Gregorievitch, a Croat critic and journalist. The three men dislike each other and they argue constantly. West and her husband see the sights of Zagreb, and engage in intellectual conversations in the cafes. They visit the village of Shestine and two castles in the country during Easter. Then, they return to Zagreb and visit the cathedral. West interweaves the travelogue with the turbulent story of Croatian history. Oppressed by the Austro-Hungarian empire, Croats had rarely known peace and security, and West regards the Austrian influence to have had very bad effects. She also reports on the fragile state of Croatian politics. Valetta fights for free speech and a free press, but the undemocratic forces are in control of the government.

Dalmatia

West and her husband travel south by train to Dalmatia on the Adriatic coast. West observes that Dalmatia has changed hands many times over hundreds of years and has known little stability. They visit the isle of Rab, and West declares it to be one of the most beautiful places in the world. She admires the people of Dalmatia because they resisted the Ottoman Empire and so "saved" the West from Islam. In Split, she admires the Roman architecture and discusses the Roman emperor Diocletian. West and her husband then visit Trogir, Korchula, and Dubrovnik. In spite of its beauty,

West does not like Dubrovnik.

Herzegovina

Herzegovina is a Slav province, which, according to West, has suffered great degradation like Bosnia and Macedonia through being subjected to Turkish rule. West and her husband visit the market at Trebinye, which is full of Muslims, descendants of the Slavs who were converted by the Turks. Then they visit an old Turkish house where an elderly man in a frock-coat gives them a very exaggerated account of the historic value of the house. As they are driving out of the town, West and her husband have one of their many discussions about politics and history. They then visit the small Muslim town of Mostar.

Bosnia

They visit Sarajevo, where they meet up again with Constantine. West admires the men and women she sees, both Christian and Muslim, and comments on relations between the sexes. She also gives an account of the history of Sarajevo, which fell into Turkish hands in 1464. It was freed from the Turks in 1878, only to fall under the rule of Austria. The main focal point of this section of the book is West's account of the events leading up to the assassination of the Austrian Archduke Franz Ferdinand and his wife in Sarajevo on June 28, 1914. The assassination prompted Austria to declare war on Serbia, which led quickly to World War I.

West describes the unsavory character of Ferdinand, redeemed only by his love for his wife, Sophie Chotek. Ferdinand stupidly visited the city on St. Vitus's day, a Serb day of celebration, when he knew Serbs regarded him as an enemy. West describes the plot against him by Serbian nationalists, and the assassin, Gavrilo Princip.

Serbia

In Belgrade, West, her husband, and Constantine are joined by Constantine's German wife, Gerda. West and her husband are offended by Gerda's rudeness. West does not find Belgrade attractive, and complains about the lavish government display which coexists with an impoverished professional class. They go sightseeing to local monuments and to a group of monasteries at Frushka Gora. One of the monasteries contains the mummified remains of Tsar Lazar, who led the Serbs to a famous defeat against the Turks in 1389. West goes on to describe the history of Serbia (culminating in the Balkan War in 1912, in which the Serbs defeated the Turks) and the tragedy of World War I. After World War I, King Alexander tried to forge a unified state out of the mix of Serbs, Croats, and Slovenes. In 1929 he abolished political parties and declared a dictatorship. He was assassinated in 1934.

Macedonia

West admires Macedonia as the repository of a

"supremely beautiful" Byzantine civilization. She and her husband visit a succession of churches and monasteries; they go to a Turkish pasha's palace at Bardovtsi, and they examine the frescoes in a Byzantine church in Neresi. At Ochrid they meet Bishop Nikolai, who strikes West as the most remarkable human being she has ever met. They visit Kaimakshalan, the mountain where the Serbs drove out the Bulgarians in World War I. But the most significant scene occurs when they go to a ceremony on St. George's Eve and watch the sacrifice of a lamb in a fertility rite. West regards this as shameful and repulsive.

Old Serbia

West, her husband, and Constantine visit the great plain at Kossovo, where the Serbs were defeated by the Turks in 1389. Kossovo strikes her as desolate and full of tragedy, the population steeped in misery. She visits a church at Grachinatsa, forty miles from the battlefield, which displays many valuable aspects of Serb culture that were destroyed after the Turkish conquest. She describes Serbian history during the pre-1389 period, emphasizing the life of Stephen Dushan (died 1365), a king who built an empire and made Serbia great. Constantine recites the folk-poetry about the battle of Kossovo, and West sees its credo of sacrifice as immensely significant.

Montenegro

West reviews the history of Montenegro and calls it a prison because its people are locked up in centuries-old ideas about heroism involving slaughter and victory. On a mountainside, West meets and is inspired by an old woman who is struggling to understand her own tragic life. Inspiration turns to horror when West and her husband climb a steep mountain, only to find that their local guide is lost. The guide insists that they make a dangerous descent down a track on the other side of the cliff. When they manage to return the way they came, they learn that the guide risked their lives simply because he did not want to admit he was lost.

Epilogue

West reviews the significance of her knowledge of Yugoslavia up to 1941, in light of World War II. She comments on the nature of empires and on the causes of the rise of Hitler in Germany and Mussolini in Italy. West has bitter words for the policy of appeasement practiced by the British government during the 1930s that left Britain unprepared for the approaching war with Germany. She makes a parallel between 1930s Britain and the way the Serbs were defeated by the Turks in 1389, and she warns of the terrible consequences of defeat. Finally, West has high praise for the bravery of the people of Yugoslavia, who refused to capitulate to Hitler, thus providing inspiration to the rest of beleaguered Europe.

Key Figures

King Alexander I

King Alexander I became king of Yugoslavia in 1921. He had fought in World War I and believed passionately in the ideal of a Yugoslav state. However, ethnic and political divisions within the new kingdom were acute. Croats demanded independence and there were so many political parties that stable government proved impossible. In 1929 Alexander abolished the constitution and ruled as a dictator. He was assassinated in 1934 in Marseille, France—an event that first aroused Rebecca West's interest in Yugoslavia.

Henry Andrews

Henry Andrews is Rebecca West's husband. He is an Oxford-educated banker who speaks fluent German, and he accompanies West throughout her travels. In their discussions about people, culture, and history, West presents Andrews as a man who speaks reasonably, without anger or prejudice. He is patient and full of common sense, although he and his wife do not always agree with each other.

Nedyelyko Chabrinovich

Nedyelyko Chabrinovich was one of the Serb

conspirators in the assassination of Archduke Franz Ferdinand. He threw a bomb that missed the archduke but wounded his aide-de-camp (camp assistant). Chabrinovich was sentenced to twenty years in prison.

Archduchess Sophie Chotek

Archduchess Sophie Chotek was the wife of Archduke Franz Ferdinand. There was opposition in the Austrian court to her marriage because, even though she was a countess, she was not considered noble enough to marry an archduke. After the marriage, she continued to be excluded from the most intimate functions of the Austrian court. West presents Sophie as an ambitious woman who nursed petty resentments and had many enemies. However, she and Ferdinand felt great love for each other, although she feared that her husband was on the verge of going mad. Sophie was assassinated with her husband in Sarajevo in June 1914.

Constantine

Constantine is a close friend of West and her husband. He accompanies them on most of their travels. A forty-six-year-old poet, Constantine, who is a Serb and is Jewish, lives in Serbia. He is also a member of the Orthodox church. Constantine is short and fat, with black curly hair, and he talks incessantly: "In the morning he comes out of his bedroom in the middle of a sentence; and at night he backs into it, so that he can just finish one more sentence." But his talk is very entertaining. He is emotional and excitable and sometimes boastful, with strong opinions on almost everything. Constantine fought in World War I and is now an official in the Yugoslav government. He believes firmly in the ideal of Yugoslavia. He is a passionate, cultured man who studied philosophy at the Sorbonne in Paris. He is also an accomplished musician.

Constantine is married to Gerda, whom he adores, although the German Gerda is a difficult wife. As Constantine tries to appease her, he becomes an increasingly unhappy figure. West notes that when Constantine is with Gerda, his personality changes, and he does not express himself so fully. Instead, he seems to mold himself according to his idea of what she might find acceptable. Sometimes he adopts the role of the Jewish comedian. Later in their travels, West observes that because of the influence of Gerda, Constantine has undergone a "disintegrating change," and she no longer trusts his judgment. Constantine becomes irritable and complains about everything. West concludes that there is something in Constantine's personality that compels him to be loyal only to those who despise him.

Diocletian

Diocletian was the Roman Emperor who, after a twenty-one-year reign as emperor, built a palace in 305 at Split in Dalmatia. West considers him the greatest of the Roman emperors who came from Illyria. He died, probably by poisoning himself, sometime between 313 and 316.

Dragutin

Dragutin, a Serb, is the chauffeur for West and her husband during their travels through Macedonia, Old Serbia, and Montenegro. West presents Dragutin as the embodiment of the passionate, fierce temperament of the Serbian male. Raised in both Germany and England, he is young, handsome, brave, and honest. He is also an effective tour guide and takes charge when necessary, knowing the ways of his people and the hazards of the terrain. Dragutin is strongly pro-Yugoslavia, and when his party visits the ancient battlefield at Kossovo, he shows great contempt for the Turks.

Stephen Dushan

Stephen Dushan was the monarch of the old Serbian empire during the mid-fourteenth century, when Serbia reached the height of its power and its culture flowered. West compares Dushan to Elizabeth I of England, who, like Dushan, inherited a threatened kingdom and left it a powerful one. Dushan successfully confronted the hostile Bulgaria, Bosnia, and Hungary, and had he lived longer, he might have reunited the entire Byzantine world. Dushan died at the age of forty-eight in 1365, only thirty-four years before the Serbs were defeated at Kossovo in 1389. (In modern spelling, one "s" for Kosovo is preferred, rather than West's "Kossovo".)

Archduke Franz Ferdinand

Archduke Franz Ferdinand was the nephew of Franz Joseph, Emperor of Austria. Ferdinand and his wife Sophie were assassinated in June 1914 in Sarajevo—an event that sparked World War I. West presents Ferdinand as an extremely unattractive figure. He was dull-minded, ungracious, obstinate, bigoted, suspicious, and aggressive. He loved hunting simply because he liked to kill, and he hated the entire world, with the exception of his wife and children.

Gerda

Gerda is Constantine's German wife. West and her husband meet her in Belgrade, and she accompanies them on some of their subsequent travels. Gerda is middle-aged and stout, with fair hair and gray eyes. Constantine claims she is beautiful, and he adores her, but Gerda is a thoroughly unattractive figure. She is a nationalistic German who despises the Slavs, even though she lives amongst them. In her opinion, they have no culture; they are all primitive and stupid. Gerda and West get off to a bad start when Gerda expresses contempt for the book West is carrying, even though she has never read it. Gerda is smug in her sense of her own superiority as a German, and she is determined to dislike West and her husband. Her views are compatible with the Nazis. She believes for example that all Slavs in Germany should be expelled so that the land can be given back to "true Germans."

Gerda proves to be a disagreeable traveling companion. In Skoplje, Macedonia, she disparages Byzantine art, hates West and her husband because they are English, and calls all Yugoslavs liars. She hates the Gypsy dancers, saying that Gypsies are "dirty and stupid," and she has to smoke a cigarette to "disinfect" herself from their contamination. After this episode, she insults a poor old man.

Gerda becomes so unpleasant that eventually West and her husband are forced to insist that she accompany them no further. She returns to Belgrade on her own.

Marko Gregorievitch

Marko Gregorievitch is a friend of West and her husband, whom they meet in Zagreb. He is a gloomy fifty-six-year-old Croat critic and journalist who looks like Pluto in the Mickey Mouse films. For sixteen years before World War I he was an active revolutionary, fighting the Hungarians for the right of Croatia to run its own affairs, for which he suffered imprisonment and exile. He now supports the Yugoslavian state with great enthusiasm because it symbolizes Slav defiance of the Austrian-Hungarian empire. He dislikes Valetta and regards him as a traitor.

Karageorge

Karageorge was a leader of Serbia in the early nineteenth century. He led an insurrection against the Turks in 1804. West describes him as one of the most remarkable men in European history. Although he could neither read nor write, he excelled as a soldier, strategist, and diplomat. In 1813 his career came to an disreputable end when he fled the scene of a great battle with the Turks. He later returned to Serbia but was assassinated in 1817. In spite of his failures, Serbs still regard him as the founder of their liberty.

Tsar Lazar

Tsar Lazar was the leader of the Serbs defeated by the Turks at Kossovo in 1389. West visits his tomb and touches his mummified hand.

Draga Mashin

Draga Mashin was the hated wife of Serbia's King Alexander Obrenovitch. She was born in 1866, married young, and was widowed in 1885. In 1900 she married Alexander, who was more than ten years younger than she. Draga was loathed throughout Serbia because it was said she was of low birth and had led a vicious life. West is sympathetic to Draga but concedes she may have led a loose life before her marriage. After marriage Draga was further reviled because it was believed she was unable to bear a child. She was brutally murdered along with her husband by Serbian army officers in 1903. The naked, mutilated corpses were thrown out of the window of the palace.

Bishop Nikolai

Bishop Nikolai is Bishop of Zhitcha and of Ochrid, in Macedonia. He holds an Easter service at the Church of Sveti Yovan (St. John) that West attends. She is greatly impressed by his spiritual power and charisma.

King Alexander Obrenovitch

Alexander Obrenovitch inherited the throne of Serbia in 1890, when he was twelve years old. Until the age of seventeen, he ruled through three regents. Alexander showed little wisdom in government, one of his first acts being to abolish freedom of speech and of the press. In 1900 he married the hated Draga Mashin. In 1901 he appointed a military dictatorship after a failed attempt to establish a new constitution. In 1903, with the Serbian economy in shambles, there were riots in Belgrade. A general election was held and the government falsified the results. A month later, in June 1903, a group of army officers assassinated both Alexander and his wife in their palace at night.

Gavrilo Princip

Gavrilo Princip was the Bosnian Serb nationalist who shot Archduke Franz Ferdinand to death in 1914. When he was a young man, Princip's peasant family sent him to Sarajevo to get an education and earn money. He soon dropped out of his studies and traveled to Belgrade to enroll in secondary studies. He then volunteered to fight in the Balkan war in 1913, but he was physically weak and was discharged from the army. Back in Belgrade, he met Nedyelyko Chabrinovich, who was to become one of his fellow conspirators. When he was convicted of the assassination, Princip was too young to be sentenced to death (no one under twenty-one could be executed), so he received a twenty-year prison term. In prison he did not receive the medical care he needed, and he died in 1918.

Bishop Strossmayer

Bishop Strossmayer was a great Croat patriot whose statue stands in Zagreb. Stossmayer fought for over fifty years for the liberation of Croatia from Austria-Hungary. As bishop and scholar, he campaigned for the preservation of the Serbo-Croatian language and for the right to use the Slav liturgy rather than the Latin. He also founded the University of Zagreb. He refused to have any part of the movement to persecute the Orthodox Church, because that would have set Croats against Serbs, and he also opposed anti-Semitism. West presents him as an entirely saintly human being. Strossmayer died in 1905 at the age of ninety.

Valletta

Valletta is a friend of West and her husband. A twenty-six-year-old lecturer in mathematics at Zagreb University, he is a Croat from Dalmatia, and a Roman Catholic. Unlike Constantine, he does not believe in the ideal of Yugoslavia; he is a federalist and believes Croatia should have autonomy. West considers him gentle, kind, and charming.

Rebecca West

Rebecca West is the author of the book, and Yugoslavia is seen for the most part through her eyes. She presents herself as endlessly curious and highly intellectual, with strong opinions and the ability and will to express them. She can more than hold her own in any company. Her abiding quest is to explore life in all its manifestations and understand the nature of it, its laws and purposes. She calls this "process," and sees it as a never-ending quest. She often makes sweeping statements about life, and sometimes her pronouncements are somewhat idiosyncratic, as when she says she does not like the city of Dubrovnik because its citizens appreciate the wrong kind of art.

West is an admirer of the Serbs, particularly Serbian men, and their culture. Her descriptions of Serbian history often have a romantic glow about them (the Balkan war in 1912, for example). She takes an intense interest in politics, history, and all aspects of current affairs. She is a feminist. She is also, in the 1930s, keenly aware of the threat posed by Nazi Germany and does not share the pacifist sentiments professed by many in the intellectual classes in England. She is convinced that the preservation of civilization requires a willingness to fight.

At the personal level, West has a loving relationship with her husband, although she has a tendency to give herself the last word in any of their civilized disagreements. Sometimes, however, in dealing with others she can be haughty and difficult, as when an Austrian student consults her about a dissertation she wishes to write on West's work.

West values the trivial things in life as much as the important ones—she can gain intense pleasure from a small item acquired as a bargain at a market or shop. She also appreciates fine food (and comments when necessary on the lack of it), and elegant fine manners. She is a lover and discerning critic of art and music, especially, so it seems, Mozart, and she believes in the transcendental value of art.

Themes

Sacrifice and Atonement

The main theme of the book is the damage caused in human history by the idea of sacrifice that is embedded in Christian and pagan traditions. West sees this idea working at many levels in history. Her abhorrence of it becomes clear to her in Macedonia, when she witnesses a black lamb being sacrificed on a rock in a fertility rite. She objects to the idea that the infliction of pain and death on one creature can cause another to become fertile.

West traces the idea of sacrifice to the Christian doctrine of atonement, a concept she finds repugnant. According to this doctrine, which was developed by St. Paul and refined by St. Augustine, God sacrificed His son on the cross so that man could be freed from the punishment that his sins deserved. According to West:

> This theory flouts reason at all points, for it is not possible that a just God should forgive people who are wicked because another person who was good endured agony by being nailed to a cross.

The ramifications of this doctrine have permeated Christian culture. People have been inculcated with the idea that pain and suffering is the price of anything valuable. This belief has led to the idea that there is something virtuous in being defeated, that somehow, cosmic law rewards the sacrifice of the good. West sees this idea operating in the pacifism of 1930s-Britain waiting to be the passive victim of Nazi aggression because Britons did not want to soil their hands with violence. She sees it operating also in the Serb defeat at Kossovo in 1389. To substantiate this, she refers to the epic poem commemorating the defeat, which is treasured by all Serbs. The poem relates how, before the battle, the prophet Elijah came to Tsar Lazar, the Serb leader, in the form of a grey falcon. The falcon asked Lazar what kind of kingdom he wanted—an earthly kingdom or a heavenly kingdom. If he chose the former, the falcon implied that he would be victorious, but if he chose the heavenly kingdom, he would he defeated. Lazar chose the heavenly kingdom, because a heavenly kingdom would last forever, whereas earthly kingdoms survive for only a short time. In making this choice, Lazar condemned himself to death and his army to defeat. He chose sacrifice as a means of salvation.

Empires

The theme of the destructiveness of empires runs throughout the book. Most of West's ire is concentrated on two empires: the Ottoman Empire, which subjugated the Serbs; and the Austrian Empire, chronically mismanaged by the Habsburg dynasty, which later became the Austro-Hungarian Empire and was finally destroyed as a result of

Topics for Further Study

- Research the causes of the 1999 Kosovo war. Was NATO justified in the actions it took? Were U.S. vital interests at stake? How should those interests be defined?

- Research the causes of World War I. Would the war still have happened had Archduke Franz Ferdinand not been assassinated in Sarajevo in 1914? Why or why not?

- West admired the Serbs, including Serb nationalism, which she regarded as "defensive" rather than aggressive. What is nationalism and is it a positive or negative force in the world today? Provide some examples.

- In the Bosnian war of 1992 to 1995, should the West have intervened earlier than it did to prevent the slaughters that happened there? Should the United States be responsible for ensuring that the peace agreement of 1995 is maintained? Why or why not?

- Write a character analysis of Gerda. Explain how her attitudes reflect the Nazi ideology that gripped Germany in the 1930s.

However, West, who grew up as a citizen of the British Empire at the height of its power, was not an absolute opponent of imperialism. She states that it has often proved "magnificent" in practice. An empire could spread civilization, develop technology, bring the rule of law, and tame nature. But empires are not always enlightened. In the case of the British Empire, in addition to its achievements in granting self-government to its dominions, there was hypocrisy. The Roman Empire in some respects destroyed more human achievements than it fostered. The disadvantages of empire are best illustrated in the Balkans. The Turks, according to West, despoiled Macedonia and old Serbia (which included Kossovo) and robbed its inhabitants for so long that there was almost nothing left. The same was true of Dalmatia by Venice, and

Croatia by Hungary. The history of the Balkans shows that when an empire attempts to travel too far beyond its boundaries, it is nothing but a curse to the native inhabitants.

Manichaeism

Manichaeism was a Christian heresy, which is an opinion or doctrine contrary to church dogma. According to its cosmology, there had originally been a kingdom of light and a kingdom of darkness that were quite separate from each other. The present world resulted from the aggression of the kingdom of darkness. It was the task of the virtuous to extract the sparks of light that were imprisoned in the darkness of this world. The heresy was ruthlessly suppressed by the Roman Catholic and Orthodox churches.

West discusses Manichaeism in relation to the history of Dalmatia. She regards the heresy as an extremely useful conception of life and uses it as an allegory of history. West tends to think in black-and-white terms, and she sees the Germans and Turks aligned on the dark side, and the Serbs, for the most part, as representing the light. She also sees herself as somewhat like a virtuous Manichaean living in a world full of darkness, charged with using her discriminating intellect to understand life and extract from the darkness whatever fragments of light she can discover.

Relationships between the Sexes

West writes about relations between the sexes at the personal and societal level, and describes the differences between them. She observes that men and women see totally different aspects of reality. Women are often interested only in the personal side of life and ignore the wider context of history. This weakness she calls idiocy, after the Greek root meaning "private person." Men, on the other hand, are so obsessed by public affairs that they cannot see the details correctly; they see as if by moonlight, and West calls this "lunacy."

During her travels, she sees frequent examples of the oppression of women by men. She regards the costumes of the women in Herzegovina—who wear masculine-looking coats much too large for them that can be pulled up and used as a veil—as a sign of male hostility to women. Such clothes, she says, are imposed by a male society that has neurotic ideas about female bodies and wants to insult them and drive them into hiding. Women cannot be happy in such societies. One of the reasons men oppress women is that they need to be reassured; they like to feel superior to women.

West feels compassion for the oppressed women of Macedonia. She is also angered when in Kossovo she sees a young female peasant walking with a ploughshare tied to her back, while her husband walks alongside her, carrying nothing. West is disgusted by societies where women do all the physical work, not only because of the unfair burden placed on women but because such arrangements also emasculate the men. West observes in one of her typical generalizations that men are easily discouraged. Once women have proved they can do something just as well as men, the men are reluctant to go on doing it. They either become enemies of their wives or relapse into an infantile state of dependence. This bewilders the women, who expect men to be strong.

However, at times, to the consternation of some feminist critics, West seems to accept the traditional gender roles. In a phrase that sounds somewhat old-fashioned today, she writes that in Dalmatia she encountered a world "where men are men and women are women." She is referring to the virile strength of Slavic men (in contrast to the effete men of the West). And in Bosnia, in contrast to Macedonia, she finds women who seem completely free in spirit, in spite of the fact that they must wait on their husbands, take beatings from them, and walk while the men ride. On this occasion, West offers no censure of such arrangements, even though she knows they are based on a pretense by the women—that the women accept the men's judgment that they are inferior.

Parallel to West's observations of and generalizations about relations between men and women is her own relationship with her husband, which seems a civilized and tolerant one. Their disagreements are of the intellectual kind and they discuss them in even, respectful tones. She allows her husband his eccentricities and they seem to regard each other with good humor. Each cares for the welfare of the other. As the chauffeur in

Macedonia says, touchingly, "Yes, they're fond of each other all right, look how close they are sitting and they aren't young either."

Style

Symbolism

The central symbols in *Black Lamb and Grey Falcon* are those that supply the book with its title: the black lamb and the grey falcon. The black lamb appears several times. Its first appearance is an innocent one. In a hotel in Belgrade, West watches as a peasant enters the hotel carrying a black lamb in his arms. The lamb twists and writhes, "its eyes sometimes catching the light as it turned and shining like small luminous plates." The significance of the lamb as a symbol is only made clear later in the narrative, when West attends the fertility rite on a rock in Macedonia and watches a lamb being sacrificed. She describes the process in grisly detail and then reveals the symbolic significance she attaches to it: the slaughter of the lamb represents a particular way of thinking, the idea that suffering and cruelty are not only necessary but are the only ways by which good may come forth. West prefers to see the ugliness of the ritual for what she perceives it to be. Those who practice such "beastly retrogression," claims West, do so because "they wanted to put their hands on something weaker than themselves … to smash what was whole, to puddle in the warm stickiness of their own secretions."

In a later incident, after West has visited the

ancient site of the battle of Kossovo, an Albanian man joins them to eat, and he is carrying a black lamb. The lamb unexpectedly stretches out its neck and lays its muzzle against West's forearm. She is startled and cries out. The men laugh, and she is reminded once more, because of the symbolic value she has ascribed to the lamb, of the "infatuation with sacrifice," and she admits that she herself is not free of it.

The grey falcon, which appears in the Serbs' epic poem about their 1389 defeat, represents the same ideal of sacrifice. It symbolizes Tsar Lazar's willingness to sacrifice himself and his army in exchange for a heavenly kingdom. On the battlefield at Kossovo, West remarks, the grey falcon and the black lamb worked together.

West even extends the symbolism of the lamb and the falcon to apply to the relationship between Constantine and Gerda. Constantine is the lamb. He loves Gerda innocently, wanting to serve her, even though she treats him cruelly. He has absorbed the myth of sacrifice, that it is better to be pure and loving (even if this means a personal defeat) than to involve himself in the unsavory tactics of the aggressor.

In the epilogue, West returns to the image of the grey falcon, but this time she interprets it differently. She applies it to the heroic resistance of the Yugoslavs against the Nazis in World War II, even in the face of certain defeat. The Yugoslavs, fully conscious of their great poem about Kossovo, fought on this time not because they were in love with sacrifice and death, but, on the contrary, because of their "love of life"; because they knew that, ultimately, a state based on justice would outlast one based on evil.

Digressions

The book does not have a clearly delineated structure. Passages describing West's travels—which include delightful nature descriptions, scenes in restaurants and cafes, and visits to churches and monuments—jostle alongside long and colorful accounts of the troubled history of the Balkans. At any point, triggered by some observation of the scene or a conversation, West is likely to digress about one of her many pet topics. Often she sees deep significance in small details, and a particular incident may prompt her to make sweeping generalizations about life.

For example, when a doctor at a sanatorium in Croatia tells her that the sanatorium sends patients home heavier than when they came in (because they feed them well), West makes a generalization that is also a comparison between Slavs and Westerners: "These people hold that the way to make life better is to add good things to it, whereas in the West we hold that the way to make life better is to take bad things away from it." This type of statement is known as an aphorism: a concise statement of a principle. There are many more aphorisms in the book. "It is not comfortable to be an inhabitant of this globe," West says as she contemplates Croatian history. Few would argue with this statement, but sometimes West's aphorisms are more idiosyncratic: "All women believe that some day something supremely agreeable will happen, and that afterwards the whole of life will be agreeable."

Sometimes West's observations lead her to an epiphany. The term epiphany is used by literary critics to refer to a revelation of some profound truth or vision that is prompted by an ordinary object or scene. William Wordsworth's poem, *The Prelude* (1850), for example, is full of epiphanies, and there are several in West's book. The most striking is when, in Montenegro, West encounters an old peasant woman walking on a mountain road. The woman tells West that she (the woman) is not going anywhere; she walks about only to seek understanding of her tragic life, of why it took the form it did. West admires her because she does not simply accept her fate; she attempts to understand what West calls "the mystery of process," which is the sole justification of all art and science. The woman inspires West to believe that at some point in the future "we will read the riddle of our universe. We shall discover what work we have been called to do, and why we cannot do it." Only then, West says, will we be able to face our destiny.

Historical Context

The history of the Balkans is long and complex. The Slavs first entered the region in the sixth century, and by the medieval period, the Slavic group known as Serbs had established a formidable kingdom, including the areas now known as Macedonia and Montenegro. But the Turks defeated them in 1389 and the Ottoman Empire then dominated the region. Many Serbs in Bosnia converted to Islam. Most of Croatia (Croats are also Slavs) fell first under the influence of Hungary and then of Austria-Hungary. Most of Croatia remained Roman Catholic; the Serbs were Orthodox Christians.

In the nineteenth century Serbia began to shake off Turkish rule, culminating in the Congress of Berlin in 1878, under which the Serbs gained their independence. But the same congress gave Bosnia and Herzegovina to Austria-Hungary. Macedonia was freed from Turkish rule in 1913, most of it being awarded to Serbia.

In 1918, after World War I, a new state was formed, officially called the Kingdom of the Serbs, Croats, and Slovenes. It consisted of Serbia, Bosnia, Croatia, Dalmatia, Slovenia, Montenegro, and Macedonia. Within Serbia, Kosovo was created as an autonomous province, because of its largely Muslim population.

From the outset, it was difficult to forge unity amongst such a multiethnic people. There were also differences in religion. Croats and Slovenes were Roman Catholics; Serbs and Montenegrins were Orthodox Christians; and a large proportion of Bosnians were Muslims.

A constitution was created in 1921 that established a constitutional monarchy operating within a centralized system based in Belgrade, the Serbian capital. From 1921 to 1929 the new state functioned as a parliamentary democracy, dominated by Serbia. However, there was continuing hostility between Serbs and Croats and an ongoing debate about the desirability of central control. This is amply reported in *Black Lamb and Grey Falcon*, especially in the early chapters set in Zagreb, Croatia, in which Valetta is the spokesman for an independent Croatia. He regards government from Belgrade as a tyranny. He is opposed by Constantine, who supports the Yugoslavian state.

In 1928 a delegate from Montenegro shot five members of the Croatian Peasant Party. Faced with a severe crisis in the country, King Alexander I abolished the constitution and declared a dictatorship. He also renamed the state Yugoslavia (Yugoslav means "South Slav"). Alexander was assassinated in 1934, and, after his death, Yugoslavia was ruled by a three-man regency, since Alexander's son was only eleven years old.

During the late 1930s, when West made her trips to Yugoslavia, the storm clouds of war were gathering once more over Europe. In September 1939, Germany invaded Poland, and World War II began. In 1940 Germany asked Yugoslavia to sign the Axis Tripartite Act. This act would have caused Yugoslavia to be enslaved by the Axis powers of Germany and Italy. Yugoslavia's pro-German government signed the agreement, but two days later the government was overthrown by an army coup that had the support of the Yugoslav people. In *Black Lamb and Grey Falcon*, West gives a vivid account of these events, presenting the Yugoslav people as united in their desire to resist the Nazis: "The passions of the people blazed up into a steady flame.… The whole country demanded that … arms must be taken up against the Germans." In April 1941, Germany declared war on Yugoslavia, and eleven days later the Yugoslavs were defeated.

During the war, thousands of Serbs were sent to concentration camps and killed. In Croatia, the Germans put the fascist Ante Pavelic and his Ustasa forces in charge. In *Black Lamb and Grey Falcon*, West describes Pavelic as a terrorist who was responsible for the deaths of many people and who supplied the assassins of King Alexander with weapons. When Pavelic gained power in Croatia, he ruthlessly persecuted the Serbs living in Croatia and Bosnia, as well as gypsies and Jews. Many were sent to their deaths in concentration camps, such as the one at Jasenovac, southeast of Zagreb.

In the meantime, resistance movements against the Germans were formed in Yugoslavia, and they carried on guerrilla campaigns. The most successful of these movements was led by the Partisans, a communist group headed by Josip Broz Tito. In 1944 Partisan and Russian forces took Belgrade.

After World War II ended in 1945, Yugoslavia was reestablished as a communist state under the rule of Marshal Tito.

Critical Overview

When published in 1941, *Black Lamb and Grey Falcon* received high praise but also some criticism. *Time* magazine (quoted in Wolfe) called it "one of the most passionate, eloquent, violent, beautifully written books of our time." Katherine Woods, in the *New York Times Book Review,* regarded it as "the magnification and intensification of the travel book form," and added that it was "carried out with tireless percipience, nourished from almost bewildering erudition, chronicled with a thoughtfulness itself fervent and poetic." Clifton Fadiman in the *New Yorker* thought it "as astonishing as it is brilliant … it is also one of the great books of our time."

Compare & Contrast

- **1930s:** The independent state of Yugoslavia includes Serbia, Bosnia, Croatia, Slovenia, Montenegro, Macedonia, and Dalmatia.

  Today: Following the breakup of Yugoslavia after the fall of communism, and a series of wars in the 1990s, Yugoslavia consists of Serbia and Montenegro only. Bosnia, Croatia, Macedonia, and Slovenia are independent nations.

Kosovo, although still officially part of Serbia, is under the jurisdiction of the North Atlantic Treaty Organization (NATO) following the conflict between Serbia and NATO in 1999.

- **1930s:** The Nazi party under Adolf Hitler takes power in Germany. Hitler bans all other political parties and brings economic and cultural life under the control of the central government. The persecution of non-Aryans begins. The Nuremberg Laws of 1935 deprive Jews of their German citizenship and forbid marriage between Jews and Aryans. More anti-Semitic laws are passed over the next few years. Hitler's rearmament of Germany and his aggressive, expansionist foreign policies lead to World War II.

  Today: Germany, divided into East Germany and West Germany after World War II, is reunited (since 1990), and is a democratic nation that is a member of the European Union and NATO.

- **1930s:** The world is dominated by competing political ideologies of socialism, fascism, and communism. In much of Europe, this is an age of totalitarianism, in which the state has power over many aspects of individual life. Totalitarianism is on the rise because, with the coming of the Great Depression in the United States, capitalism appears to be a failed system. Many in Europe are attracted to new systems that seem to hold out a promise of full employment and greater social equality.

Today: As political systems, communism and socialism are on the wane throughout the world. Only a few countries still have communist governments, including North Korea, Cuba, and China. Because capitalism and parliamentary democracy have had greater success in providing economic prosperity and political freedom, these systems are being adopted by an increasing number of nations. International terrorism presents a greater threat to world stability than conventional war between nation-states.

Other reviewers took West to task for an over-romanticized view of the virtues of Serb culture. In the *New Republic* (quoted in Rollyson, *Rebecca West: A Life*), Nigel Dennis wrote that the book was a "retelling of a tale we know all too well; the quest of the frustrated Western intellectual for a Nirvana of vitality and self-expression."

Later critics often refer to *Black Lamb and Grey Falcon* as West's masterpiece. Peter Wolfe calls it her "biggest and boldest work" containing some of her best prose. Wolfe characterized the work as a "modern epic," pointing to the following elements in the book: "coursing back and forth over long stretches of time, the many characters, the battle scenes, the ritual sacrifices, the trip to the underworld of a Serbian mine shaft, the founding of a new world order, and Balkan heroism over the centuries."

Wolfe also argues that the book has a unified structure, the first part revolving around the assassination of Archduke Franz Ferdinand in 1914, and the second part focussing on the defeat of the Serbs at Kosovo in 1389.

In *The Literary Legacy of Rebecca West,* Carl Rollyson describes the book as an exemplification of what West called "process," which he defines as "the mind's ability to think through the stages by which it comes to know itself and the world." Rollyson also notes that in addition to being a travelogue and history, the book is also West's "spiritual autobiography."

Harold Orel notes how West's sense of an impending war between Germany and England shaped and colored her narrative. Orel argues that the book is not unified by any literary structure. He prefers to see it as a "spider's web," in which all the separate elements lead to many different connections, "larger generalizations, greater truths, than the conventional writer of a travel journal can imagine."

During the Balkan wars of the 1990s, *Black Lamb and Grey Falcon* attracted fresh attention not from literary critics but from a new generation of journalists and commentators on current affairs who sought to understand the region that once again had drawn the Western powers into armed conflict. As of the beginning of the twenty-first century, *Black Lamb and Grey Falcon* is regarded as an indispensable source of knowledge and insight into the former Yugoslavia, as well as essential to an understanding and appreciation of West's work as a whole.

What Do I Read Next?

- In West's first novel, *The Return of the Soldier* (1918), a shell-shocked soldier returns from World War I in 1916 having lost his memory of everything that happened to him over the previous fifteen years. The novel analyzes the lives of three women who are emotionally connected to him.

- *The Balkans: Nationalism, War & the Great Powers, 1804-1999* (2001), by Misha Glenny, is a history of the Balkans, showing how it has long suffered at the hands of the great powers that surround it. Glenny is highly critical of NATO's 1999 war against Serbia over Kosovo.

- *Kosovo: A Short History* (1999), by Noel Malcolm, a British historian and journalist, provides the troubled history of the province where conflict between Serbs and ethnic Albanians led to the 1999 NATO intervention.

- *Kosovo: War and Revenge* (2000), by Tim Judah, is an account of the 1999 Kosovo war by a journalist who covered it as it was happening.

- Like *Black Lamb and Grey Falcon, Balkan Ghosts: A Journey through History* (1994), by journalist Robert D. Kaplan, is a travelogue deeply imbued with the political history of the Balkans. Kaplan sees the major players in the Balkan wars of the 1990s as reincarnations of aspects of the violent history of the region going back six hundred years.

- *Zlata's Diary: A Child's Life in Sarajevo* (1995), by Zlata Filipovic, translated by Christina Pribichevich-Zoric, is a diary kept by eleven-year-old Filipovic from 1991 to 1993 in Sarajevo. Her childhood was disrupted by the terror of war as Bosnian Serbs besieged the city. She endured years of misery, fear, and deprivation.

- D. H. Lawrence admired Mexican Indian culture as much as West admired Serb culture. In his book *Mornings in Mexico* (1927), he writes of his travels in Mexico with the same kind of passion and insight that West brought to her Yugoslavian adventures.

Sources

Fadiman, Clifton, "Review," in the *New Yorker,* October 25, 1941.

Orel, Harold, *The Literary Achievement of Rebecca West,* Macmillan, 1986, pp. 164-207.

Rollyson, Carl, *The Literary Legacy of Rebecca West,* International Scholars Publications, 1998, pp. 127-67.

———, *Rebecca West: A Life,* Scribner, 1986.

Wolfe, Peter, *Rebecca West, Artist and Thinker,* Southern Illinois University Press, 1971, pp. 130-48.

Woods, Katherine, "Review," in the *New York Times,* October 26, 1941, p. 4.

Further Reading

Deakin, Motley, *Rebecca West,* Twayne, 1980.

> This is a concise survey of West's work in all genres. Deakin considers West to be a "voice of sanity" during the turbulent events of the twentieth century.

Hall, Brian, "Rebecca West's War," in the *New Yorker,* April 15, 1996, pp. 74-80, 82-83.

> Hall notes that, because the Balkans are once more in turmoil, interest in *Black Lamb and Grey Falcon* has increased. He gives a very insightful analysis of the main elements of the book.

Scott, Bonnie Kime, ed., *Selected Letters of Rebecca West,* Yale University Press, 2000.

> West was a prolific letter writer, and this volume contains hundreds of her letters, all annotated by the editor.

Tillinghast, Richard, "Rebecca West and the Tragedy of Yugoslavia," in *New Criterion,* Vol. 10, No. 10, June 1992, pp. 12-22.

> This is a discussion of West's book in the light of the disintegration of modern Yugoslavia.

Weldon, Fay, *Rebecca West,* Viking, 1985.

Weldon is a novelist, and this is an imaginative biography of West that examines her love affair with H. G. Wells. Weldon admits she invented a lot of material.